BROKEN TEETH
TONY BIRCH

Other books by Tony Birch

PROSE
Blood
Common People
Father's Day
Ghost River
Shadowboxing
The Promise
The White Girl

TONY
BIRCH

Broken Teeth

First printed in 2016
by Cordite Publishing Inc.

PO BOX 393
Carlton South 3053
Victoria, Australia
cordite.org.au

Tony Birch and Stephen Muecke assert their rights to be known as the respective author and introducer of this work.

National Library of Australia
Cataloguing-in-Publication:

Birch, Tony
Broken Teeth
978-0-9752492-2-2 paperback
I. Title.
A821.3

Poetry set in Spectral 10 / 14
Cover design by Zoë Sadokierski
Text design by Kent MacCarter and Zoë Sadokierski
Printed and bound by McPherson's Printing, Maryborough, Victoria.

Cover collage is detail from Xray by James Heilman, CC BY-SA 3.0; detail from engraving 'Mouth and teeth prosthetics', public domain via Vintage Printable and detail from 'Red Necked Fruit-Bat', 1894. Art and Picture Collection, The New York Public Library.

10 9 8 7 6 5

For my first grandchild, Isabel Kit

CONTENTS

PREFACE

I wrote many poems before I published a single word of fiction, short or long. Some of the poems I was happy with. Others were terrible. Thankfully, most of the bad stuff was never published, although a couple of the more atrocious ones were. I hope they're being taught somewhere as examples of bad writing and giving students a laugh. The poems of mine that I'm most happy with, while not being 'found' poems, riff off the political words of others, hammered into shape with anger, and sometimes caressed with love. Other institutional words, phrases and sentences I picked up along the way, interrogating them until they confessed their hidden meaning. Any dictatorship worth its violent salt executes the poets first. It is the way it should be, as a great poem cuts through the crap and goes for the heart and heat like a double-barrelled shotgun.

INTRODUCTION

Don't think you'll get away with lightly reading these Tony Birch poems. They are not just words whistling on the wind. They come laden with other gifts. With a whole place: Melbourne. With a long history: from before the bay filled with water, from after whitefellas came in boats and called it Port Phillip, through to today when others desperately try to reach Australian shores. The refugees' boats, the poet tells us, are still made from trees that were once earthbound, but stretching upwards. Then, like poems, they are laid down and recomposed for voyaging.

Few writers love their hometown as ardently as Birch. Read his novels and stories, look at his photographs, listen to him tell tall stories about it, run with him along the contours of its creeks, or stroll with him in the Melbourne cemetery to chat with the dead. It makes you long to '… rest along the / bluestone gutter …'. That hard, polished bluestone that cobbles the back lanes of Melbourne. They are the half-secret byways where Fitzroy kids can escape, play footy, get up to mischief and hiss a warning about the 'toe-cutters'.

Sound parochial? Sure, the inner city is Birch's local run and his knowledge runs deep. But the arc of reference is greater than for many whose compassion is not tested by suffering. You can be inner-city and global at the same time, and refuse the kind of insularity forged by fence-building for property protection. The elegy for our Japanese friend, Minoru Hokari, who jumped the fence between anthropology and history to make a journey with the Gurindji, still makes me want to weep each time I read it. And 'Michael', who I didn't know, and the boat people who no one in Australia knows. They will find a welcome in this poetry that understands how to express sovereignty without border protection.

Birch also delves into another place where things are half-concealed, the documentary archives. They turn up the most poignant letters from earlier days when, for Aboriginal Australians, even moving around was a trial or a life-threatening experience. The pages from the archive are here turned, and once again recomposed. Or 'The True History of Beruk [William Barak] (archive box no. 3)' spills the history of William Beruk, and this remarkable text goes on to experiment with lists of objects and with prose.

Objects proliferate in 'The Anatomy Contraption' sequence, where, in a singular assemblage of technology, modern science and early- twentieth-century eugenicism it is easy to coolly dissect 'three infant hearts' for a cabinet of curiosities, which 'congeals together / like a song'. It makes you wonder what elements must thus congeal to sustain the songs, the poems, across all these pages without once faltering, without missing a beat. Perhaps it is in what they call 'tone' – no pun intended, mate. What is 'it'? A combination of sounds, feelings and meanings (you can't afford to sound flippant, insincere or, if sincere, not earnest); it's such a fine line! The right tone is what makes these poems happy with themselves in this space they now inhabit, hovering between performance and reception. Birch is not immaterial in this composition – he forges it, and gets the tone right by having a felicitous and easy-going relationship with resonant words bearing honest feelings and just thoughts.

—Stephen Muecke

BROKEN TEETH

A Tree and a Boat

In the time before the bay all boats were trees. They stood end on end, settling into earth and touching air. The boats grew in the mountains and lined river valleys. In the time before the bay the feet of boats left the earth and lay and rested on stone and waited to be called to the water. They were called and drifted from rivers born in the mountains. They navigated a web of waterways working to the sea and met where the mouth of the ancient river announced its arrival to the ocean. When the time came for new life the boats provided the hollows for newborn and the cribs for nests. And when it was time for death they cocooned the spirit and journeyed the spirit home. When the ghosts first came they arrived in boats that were once also trees that had always been boats, listening to be called and shaped. When men and women came in iron chains, cutting skin and bone, with children dying in the arms of mothers, they came in boats groaning with sadness and anger. And when the boats sent themselves to the bottom of the sea, they took the ghosts, the men and women and babies with them. They are there, ready for us, resting in coffins that are also trees. Today, when the desperate come to us for sanctuary, they do not come in boats made of iron and machine. They come in boats of wood collapsing under the weight of life. The boats are speaking and they have questions for us. They want to know – are we truly human? Or, something less than we claim to be? Are we willing to lift the desperate from water and carry them to safety? Or will we send them away? The boats are here to remind us that they were here before us. And when we are gone they will stand end on end, speaking truth with the earth.

Broken

we live at 56
behind a tumble
of splintered bones
and dirty mouths
of broken teeth

low-rent tenants treasuring
a symphony of creaks
a delta of plaster cracks
knock-kneed plumbing
well swept rat holes
and rising damp racing

behind my childhood home
lino discards quilt
from fence to rusting fence
where brave perfumed roses
seduce abandoned mongrels crooning
love songs to wandering drunks

at no. 56 the back fence collapses
into bluestone laneways
an escape hatch slipped through
on warm nights and weekends
to where shoeless feet
hit the ground running

Traces

a temple of fingers
bare to the bone
scratches the night

while birds of migrations
from the north of earth
breathe the spent day

a pleasure garden exile
the fruit-bat all beauty in
charcoal and chocolate

suffers its death-house tango
in a cask of plastics, shards
rusting umbilical wire and weeds

traces meet here
at the midden of civilisation
car batteries, spray-cans

and stains on a mattress
gather and pray in the stagnation
of tar and rotting papier-mâché

salvation unwinds from the shadows
in an arc by dancing sway
of silver, rouge, deep blue

when NUKE 2002
stakes a claim on
this fractured drain

Chroming

in shadows of the bridge
listing with rust red girders
hands and glances metal stained
fisting plastic bags and silver linings

boys who yesterday caressed the lips
of foaming surf
whipped sleek bodies
with tanned straps of kelp

hobble in scabbed and scare-crowed
on empty pockets
their reminder of saving's grace
a scrawled scrap

of paper we drift below
the city together sharing fumes
the bliss of avoiding eye contact
we seek nothing of each other

Creek and Kite

we were children
robbed of music, water
air & blood

the creek
a barb-wired heart
beat us hot

the black kite
dips a wing
shifts her path

rests on blue
shaping the sky
her own

water follows this time
fence follows line
sunlight tinny

& the wind sounds
crackle & spark
in skirts of grass

Dead City

I.

Colonial sapphire the south
a playground all columns
and quarried stone
a fix seeping with gold
leaves tastes on the tongue
and a nagging itch
on the city's skin

500 tongues sounded like the sky
when the civilised 'cometh'
bearing Bible tracts
and churches' bells
knelling alongside skulls
our dead swayed
and the preachers rejoiced
in Amen

beneath foundation stones
the hushed consecration
of spirited bodies lay
together with blood and hair
and bone regenerating as one

II.

the city unravels in a daze
of lights and party tricks
citizens trip on plastic chips
a red-black/ red-black marble rave
gamblers rest in stained suits
collapsing into vertiginous fits and catatonic dribbles

the Victorian city of night
in when the land craves sleep
a dragon's thankyou hovers
at the water's edge
a river snaking
to a thunder-clap heartbeat
while the washed away wait
to come forward in deluge

Visiting

I trace lives along the river; below the Cat-Walk where we hung as sleeping bats from the rusting beams we left above to fall through summer heat, readying for the touch of velvet waters dammed sixty feet below. We lifted the skirts of Skipping Girl, strobing her night vent with an erratic neon, one lighting the banks infested with years of boosted car wrecks and wet lovers, until the day came to dress the Girl and order her to perform the peak-hour crawl, homeward bound to emptiness. The river's edge is beautified now, bridges caged in safety, Deep Rock lies drowned beneath a strip of freeway and long-abandoned sweat shops dazzle with the cheapness of glass in steel. Sitting at the falls I skip stones to conjure a memory of you and see us here on summer nights. Together we carried the river home with us, in our hair and on our skin.

With Rebecca

Walking the creek we think about rubbish and our footsteps wading through weeds, and we talk about children and husbands and wives, what is lost that can never be recovered and what it is we have that will never be lost, and that we can chat about football and why we love it and why we hate it, we talk about art, sing songs and compose poems in our heads. We meet people along the bank, killing snakes, necking rabbits and adoring their hardy dogs and kids in tow. We sit and share our lunch and more about kids, and we worry over the environment and on meeting the people setting fire to land in the hope of nurturing it, and we say goodbye to each other in the late afternoon, knowing that we have to do something while never understanding what that something might be. And at the end of the day, when the stars come out, not giving up on us, the only gift we have, all we can do, all we can ever do, you, me and the kids and the dogs, is breath in and breath out. Again.

A Songline for Minoru

A dark track of blood
leads to the crematorium
I feel myself lost along a boundary
weave of hard wire
drifting away in my thoughts of you

I stay with our light
resting with my shoulder
a warmth has come to meet me
it is Mino telling me to hold on
within this quiet moment
his journey home

in the wooden boat
you lay yourself out
resting eyelids, lips and heart
sleeping quietly in your song
the shroud of skin builds
to ease your body from home
                              to home

                    a home

you've left and carry with you
the land of our loved children
touching your soles
and lifting the flight of your kin
we send you away on your
new song, your companion
its voice circles to us
to where all we know
we know more of now
through the beauty of you
Mino, our friend, loved friend
we will meet with you
in the rhythm of this song
as it sways your life within each of us:

      Mino is here
      when we come
      to speak with others
      to call to ourselves
      he is with us

      when we rest
      he is us

      Mino is here
            Mino is here
            Mino

PART

RAZOR WIRE NATION

Mahzar

the sag of your breath
a flutter of heart
taps a niggling beat
the back door of the nation
at your kid glove touch
caresses vernix skin
finger shadows dance
loops of naïve pleasure
while blood moves through
a body so resembling love lives
already known

in kitchens and cafes
on barking streets
we wake to birds soaking the early day
and a choir of espresso machines
shaking at the edge of enjoyment
buried in a recess of shame
where our conscience fails
we drown in the volume of a mantra
to this morning

'Mahzar Bakhtiyari
you cannot be
cannot be
you cannot be'

(born in Adelaide, 15 October 2003, 'in a hospital room temporarily designated as a detention zone')

Footnote to a History War (archive box no. 2)

(i)

they are nearer white
than half-caste &
are but idle bodies

irresponsible, hopeless &
worthless, they are
a drain for our goodwill

insolent & defiant
they will not respond
to our kindness

or our care

(ii)

we are sorry
to trouble your souls
with our sickness

we suffer influenza
typhoid & sores
we suffer, Amen

also, we're late
to wish for you respectfully
a most Happy New Year

better late than never

(iii)

he is one pure
aboriginal man
of good behaviour

he carries a rancid leg
its cure is medicine
& regular ration

he is sober & steady
a good working man
by a hard working day

who carries a rancid leg

(iv)

my colour debars me
my child is dead
& I am lost

we are broken into parts
our home left in the wind
& it grows colder here

my wife is aborigine
I am half-caste
and I am, Sir, dutifully yours

I await your response

(v)

he wears a suit [issue no.6]
hat [issue no.7] & possesses
one pair of blankets

she has on loan
one mullet net &
two perch nets

their children are gone:
one [toxaemia]
one [pneumonia]

one [ditto]

(vi)

I am nearly bootless
& my colour a curse
[too white, too dark]

I am to be recommended
within unit 4, [sub file 3]
for licence renewal

I am to be approved by you
via certificate [no. 71]
herewith in this body

within me, within me

(vii)

in the name of the Lord
we are servants of Christ
called as Apostles to Him

Praise be the Lord
& the Gospel of God
the Word of the Testament

Brothers and Sisters
of the dark races
at prayer with Christ

become pure in the Lord, Amen

(viii)

we are in need
of a flannel, blanket
towel, hat & wire

1 shirt [white]
1 trousers [working]
1 tweed suit

needle & cotton
1 nightdress &
1 chemise

we are, of course, obliged

(ix)

desire to report
half-caste child
5 years of age

passed away
3 o'clock it was
just yesterday, of:

whooping cough
cerebral phlegm
& bronchitis

in the service of His Majesty

(x)

I seek with words
your gratitude
& kindness

to see my wife
my children
across the still water

I seek to touch
my daughter's
skin & heart

I ask only this from you

The True History of Beruk [William Barak] (archive box no. 3)

'My Words', Beruk (Ngamajet) – 1835

Captain Cook landed white jacket
and brass buttons Buckley
stood all raggedy
and possum skin at Muddy Creek
Batman came looking too glass
and beads and powder
in a boat around the sea

Buckley spoke his tongue
the visitor is not ghosting
look at Batman's face
do not touch his skin
his bread, his house
repeat, do not touch his house

white fellow shoot us
down like kangaroo
white fellow come
by and by white fellow come
and shoot us
shoot us down

Coranderrk – 1866

(i)

30 April, 1866

[Cost of stealing land from and incarcerating 'the blacks']

Flour	108,610	lbs.
Tea	2,991	lbs.
Sugar	28,617	lbs.
Tobacco	1,983	lbs.
Rice	3,024	lbs.
Oatmeal	450	lbs.
Soap	3,181	lbs.
Meat	787	lbs.
Blankets	1,175	pairs.
Serge shirts	548	
Twill shirts	464	
Jumpers (boys)	183	
Petticoats	424	
Chemises	111	
Tomahawks	142	
Pint pots	180	
Quart pots	100	

'The condition of the station is eminently satisfactory'

(ii)

And in that year the Protector celebrated. 'The blacks' had become, if
not civilised, 'very interesting, social and industrious'. They decorated
the tolerably well-furnished, neatly swept and very comfortable huts
with pictures taken from the London Illustrated News.

'Here,' proclaimed the Protector, pointing a finger in the direction
of the gates of Buckingham Palace, 'your mother, the Queen of Victoria,
she watches over you.' And that night the Protector wrote 'they are no
longer savages,' evidenced via the ledger of productivity:

> two little children read simply and clearly
> fourteen males and four females read from the bible
> fifteen boys and eleven girls are in the schoolhouse
> seven acres of land fenced in
> two acres of oat, three of potatoes
> three bullocks, five cows and one calf died
> six huts built
>
> working men receive [each week] sugar, 2 lbs; tea, 3oz.; flour,
> 5lbs.; tobacco, 1 fig.

There are additionally several deceased natives [including some
children] – but we rejoice to conclude that William Barak of the
Yarra Yarra tribe, married [in Christianity] Annie, of the Lower
Murray.

Coranderrk – 1881

And so William was put on a coach for Melbourne, carrying his son, David, in his arms. When they arrived at Richmond they were left in the dark and cool, and late into the night. William arrived with nothing – was left with nothing – and carried the boy to his heart through the streets where heavy brick and stone covered the footsteps of William's father and the footsteps of his own childhood. David clung to his father, William stayed with his son. When the boy was dead, William was returned to Coranderrk; welcomed home to a manager's offering consisting of dry bread and tea. And later, when William appeared before the governors to tell the story of his own people, to tell the story of his loved son, David, all that they could say, these sombre suited civil servants, was, 'Was it a wild country when you were born? Are you too old to work? [and] Do you get undershirts?' William did not know his age, but was sure that he had worked hard for these men – all for his freedom – and now his son was dead. And these men, who stayed now with William, they knew nothing of the boy – David's skin with William's skin – his name murmured on a song, William's lips, his spirit sweeping through the body of his father.

'Painting by King Billy: Last of the Yarra Tribe' – 1890

William paints with a soft voice. He paints in Prussian, rouge and charcoal – the emu, the serpent, the dancing men, the women in cloaks. William paints for God. He sees the future and paints the past for a man who goes by the name of Private Collection. He paints for the glass and stone temples of the civilised. William rests his paintbrush and poses in a starched white suit – William resting with hands in pockets for the lens. The caption reads – 'William, the friend of the white men – with white men friends, all smiling'. William hunts. William dances. William tells a story. 'I will be all gone, all gone soon,' he tells them. And then William is gone. Beruk sheds his white uniform. Discards his brush. He leaves William behind. When they are sleeping Beruk walks away. They mourn him dead – William Barak, the last of his tribe. But Beruk is William no more. And he is here.

Beruk Watches Melbourne from the Sky – 1945

Half the world is a bombsite – the spoils of liberation. V is for Victory and A is for Amen, signalled to those on the move, searching for the dead, seeking a home among the rubble. The burning flesh of Europe does not smoulder in Batmania. This is a city of cold light and benign shadows. Tombstone towers reach for the sun, casting darkened skeletal frames over fields of gold reduced to a sludge of shifting grey. The veins of roadways are empty and still. Beruk follows the story of his footsteps from the mouth of the river back to Coranderrk. Beruk looks for his people – toiling in the shadow, they have become shadows also. He looks for his father. He looks for his son. Beruk searches for William and his suit. 'It is not time,' William calls to him. 'When the bed of the river rises to meet us, it will be time.'

Beruk Visits the Riverbed – 2005

Beruk moves quietly through the canyons of the city – all is stone still now. He passes the winking lights – imitating life. He listens for machines grinding to failure. Beruk observes his reflection in the ruins of glass, now inhabited by the petrified few. Women offer themselves. Men spit abuse. While dead children drift silently by, on a journey from the river to the ocean. Beruk slips into the water, beneath the heavy metals – the leaching arsenic, iron oxides, poisons and the death throws of toxic fish. He leaves the civilised to their fate. Below the monster hulls of ships, the current carries Beruk onward and down, to where the riverbed of the Wurundjeri awaits his return. Into the darkness Beruk calls – singing of his travels until his feet meet the floor of 100,000 lives once lived. In the beauty and blackness of the riverbed Beruk greets his son, David. He greets his father – the Ngamajet. They sing, with feet raise a rhythm of shifting earth:

> we will be gone
> all gone soon
> we will be gone
>
> and we will come
> we will come
> and be
>
> we will be

All for Australia

(i)

Arms of safety

come and anchor
vessels of hope
at the line of wire

but do not speak
keep voices frozen
breath closed and fall

from southern skies
sun blessed but bloodied
and burnt
into the arms of nation

(ii)

At Curtain

asylum seekers strike
hunger and wait
for signs of life

down south politicians
belch and remain
unmoved by stitched

lips with death a beat away
they rest content
the evening's entertainment

(iii)

Order by numbers 1

hope fades for 200
or 220 or 250 or more
who went to the bottom

on the 24th of, or the 25th
(or was it on the 26th) of
when they slipped away?

the nation survives
a sinking wreck
blindness our companion

(iv)

Another 113

there are another 113
800 kms off the coast
to the west of us

there are 113 to the north
113 dropping from the sky
and 113 tunnelling in

21 children, 54 women
and 38 emaciated men
are preparing to attack

(v)

Illegal migrants boom racket

boxed and trucked
in the bowels

their labour intact
bodies available
for work and pleasure

the world of the third –
a packaged and delivered
gift to the west

(vi)

All were provided with medical attention

one man stitches
memories of home
to the wall of his heart

two women dissect
freedom into 100 slices
with shards of glass

3 ACM lieutenants
shoot water cannon
at anything that moves

(vii)

Mail was not censored

barbed wire camp
in Australian bush
is now happy home

to smiling children
nursing rich tomatoes
finger painting murals

raising battery chickens
and singing in harmony
'oh we do love freedom'

(viii)

Order by numbers 2

40 k's south of civility
2 wire fences break the horizon
arc lights probe for movement

140 staff, 768 detainees
48 degrees of heat
a steel ship of the desert

1532 feet in the dust
7680 fingers tracing lines
of freedom in the sky

(ix)

Shifting exodus

off the coast of Sicily
283 drown without notice
a collision at sea

fishermen haul nets full
of words and images
carrying stories of home

bone and teeth snared
bodies stretchered and frozen
between Eurostar and track

(x)

Tasting freedom

two Iranians recaptured
walking across the desert
without shoes or sunscreen

when interviewed two men
informed hungry journalists
'we went chasing a cloud

and asked our feet
if they would like to feel
freedom greeting skin'

(xi)

Tough new line

human comforts sacrificed
for 23 men crawling through
rolls of razor wire

fetid sewer drains
blood left at a scene suggests
detainees badly slashed

those continuing to bleed
liable to conviction
and 10 years imprisonment

(xii)

Frontline Australia

we call on all white men
of military experience and
a willingness to defend

at whatever cost and vigilance
our coastlines, our cities,
our clubs, wallets & women

against the vast mass
of humanity not of us
as we know us to be

THE ANATOMY
CONTRAPTION

The Anatomy Contraption

(i)

Inside the Museum of Anatomy
we meet with bloodless surety
no distracting heartbeat
fluctuating temperatures
no smell or last beat life
exists beyond the glass doors
of anatomy, for anatomy

once sawbones
part-apothecary
one station above
the corner butcher
approached science
too exact to be
a mere skill

within the glass cubes
rows of cabinets
in the numbering and labelling
found within the

    descriptive catalogue
    of the specimens
    in this museum

the treasure of anatomy
congeals together
like a song

(ii)

This museum is guarded
by a gilded-framed
shades-of-grey portrait
the long-dead but never
forgotten Professor Wood Johns
who forever gazes pensively
through the tiled-corridor-light
and streams
toward the insignificance
of outside life

before entry we
commence instruction
this is (to be noted):

> A PRIVATE ANATOMY MUSUEM
> (for)
> ANATOMY STUDENTS ONLY

the collection held within
is sanctified by:

> RULES GOVERNING THE USE
> OF THE MUSUEM
>
> (for example)

Only students currently enrolled
in this University for courses of instruction
in anatomy at this University
have the dutiful right
to enter and use the museum
all others who desire to use the museum
must apply to the enquiry office
Level 7

any breakages should be reported
immediately to enquiry office
Level 7

(we desire the museum so we enter)

(iii)

Inside sweet silence
but for the irritation of
a nagging repetitive tick
the black-faced clock

the hooded microscopes
wait quietly to be fondled
by soft young hands
blinds are drawn, natural light prohibited
fingerprints of life
are denied their entry

skins of glass
soup-bowl half-skulls
empty waste bins
waxed wood benches
have been vacuumed of identity:

(two examples)

no. 1-2-1

a superficial dissection
the side of its head showing
the parotid gland, facial bands
coetaneous nerves of the scalp
and the musculature of face
scalp and auricle

no. 4-4-8

dissections of three infant hearts
each showing a patent ductus arteriosus

(the work of Dr. S. Scofield, 1962)

(iv)

In this Museum
there is to be:

NO SMOKING
NO EATING ALLOWED
(obviously)
DO NOT REMOVE SPECIMENS
FROM THE CABINETS

(but please observe)

THE VARIOUS ARTICULATIONS
OF THE BASE OF THE SKULL:

Dog

Lemur

Sheep

Old World Monkey

Orang-utan

Chimpanzee

Man

the knowledge
and unquestioned acceptance
of this chain of being
is a necessary prerequisite
for instruction in this museum

any dissenting views
(if articulated)
will be transferred
to Level 7

(v)

(The museum is a menagerie of):

ABNORMALITIES OF THE ARTERIES OF THE LEG

A one-eyed man returning the gaze
through the opaque
lines of partial faces
pleading with each other
an athlete's knee in search of a leg
and a pair of nicotined lungs
about to cough black bile

which after being photographed here
went on to make their debut
on an anti-smoking poster

it is said that the poisoned lungs
travelled the city
on the side of a tram
the commuters ignored
them blackened images of death
and lit up regardless
coughing up phlegm
a show of defiance
to medicine)

this museum is the panopticon
built from splices
tissue, bits and pieces
lumps, X-rays, diseases, fluids
windpipes, spinal cords and a:

SMALL BOWEL STUDY

(note the tube in the
duodenum outlining its typical C shape)

in the museum of Man
dead men and the occasional
woman
these bodies are neither
exoticised, celebrated or denigrated

they are only dead

(but)

they are unknown white-skinned
benign old men
petrified, gasping forever
a final silent breath
they are men sleeping
behind long lashes
they are men forever
unshaven with dark traces of pre-ozone
depleted sun on the backs of their wrinkled necks

tired old men
without faces, without bodies
right-side lateral men
shaved clean like newborn
a pair of shoulders worn out by life
variations of bone and wrist
an outstretched arm, a calloused hand
digits snipped clean between the halves
of garden shears

and behind each of them
in a theatre's corner
we find 'art' – an oil painting
of nineteenth century surgeons
hovering over a body
opened to a shaft of light
falling from Heaven
this work was a gift
to this institution from
another institution:

    KOL. GERMAIDE GALERIE
    den Haag, no. 1.

(vi)

Question:

    can you explain the absence of the midline aorta?

Observe:

    sagittal section of a monkey embryo

Question:

    can you describe development
    of the submandibular gland?

Observe:

        monkey heart corresponding to a human foetus at 10
        weeks gestation

        (all will be revealed)

follow the course of the left vagus nerve
over the aorta's arch
and the left superior intercostal vein
later passing to the left
posterior pulmonary plexus
you will then clearly note
the left phrenic nerve
superficial to the scalenus anterior
and passing anterior
to the internal thoracic artery

    466
    467
    468
    469

    4 foetal skeletons
    (4 escapees from a science
    fiction movie)

in 1959 Dr. I.A. Penn peeled back
a lower leg for us to observe
No. 338 is his
posterior tibial artery and nerve
please observe

please avoid the eyes of the bodiless child
to your right   do not converse with him   do
not think of him   do not be distracted from
the path of knowledge by him   he is not to be
associated with himself

(vii)

(We do apologise, as):

In the museum you may find
the occasional fabrication
a rubberised newborn
    (for instance)
lies garrotted
in a baize-lined drawer
the boy was a fashioning
    (of sorts)
of Monsieur Tramond of Paris

Tramond has left his mark
on the boy's forearm
it is inscripted
    (see)
Tramond of Paris

        (a sound is detected –
        young med students
        suited appropriately
        in white-coated props
        furiously put pencil to paper
        while hovering over Tramond's baby)

        (note):

a lower jaw – before birth
at birth – two years – about four
years – twelve years

(note):

Section A
thyroid
heart
liver
mesonephros

(note):

no. 542
sartorium-rectus fem.-capsule-
lat. cut. n.-gl. med-cl. min-
lat. fem. circ.-tensor f. l.

(note):

in the upper specimen the ribs are free
(viii)

ANATOMIE OSTEOLOGIE SCIENCES NATURELLES

these glass and mahogany cabinets house
skeletal frames of natural woman
but man cannot stand
alone the bones are fused together
with alloy nuts and bolts
manufactured by migrant workers
of the Sidchrome Company

the wire springs and
copper-weaved sheets
hold them upright
the fabricated
the artificial and unnatural
create natural man

a team of four skeletons
stand here bemused
bodies in a vacuum
one is smiling if slightly

> (a long-dead student,
> or a cleaner perhaps,
> once discovered an entry point
> and slipped him a now
> yellowing note
> 'quiet, I am loafing'
> it reads)

no. 321 informs us
that we are witnessing development
of the cranium
but do not be deceived
nothing develops here
all the components in this museum
have passed

(ANY DISENTING VIEWS MUST BE
REPORTED TO Level 7)

and still the cranium at 10 weeks
is presented
in a progressive stage of life:
occipital bone

temporal bone

semicircular canal

cochlea

Meckel's cartilage

sphenoid bone

pharynx

foramen caecum

mandible

buccal cavity

(the list begs
but only one question

who was Meckel?)

(ix)

no. 371

'foetus at 20 weeks'
was put to rest
by Dr. LS Coles on a summer morning
1960

he had toast and tea
for breakfast
kissed his wife
on the cheek
and jumped
into his two-tone two-tonne Studebaker
driving away from suburban obscurity
into the Anatomy Department
at the University

there he checked the quality
of teeth in his saw
the sharpness of his boning knife
and went to work again

> (such information is unavailable
> to those who visit the museum
> but may be found in the reflection
> of the highly polished glass)

24 years on
the baby remains
in a beautiful sleep
in a mother's womb
they are joined
on a brightly fluoro-lit
glass wall by others
the embryonic, the rubber newborn
and children

the bodies of women
are presented
only as vessels
containers within containers
housing babies
no knowledge of their lives
is presented or required

    (do these images haunt?
    there is a child here
    who does not exist
    below the neck
    she smiles softly at me
    while looking over her shoulder
    at the vivisectionist
    and his tray of sterile instruments
    her face rests against the glass)

in the museum
there are no histories
no stories
anonymity in anatomy there
is the aged grain in wood
it does not speak
there are only the dates
and names of men who acted
with such efficacy

the dead offered themselves
by roadways, riverbanks, hospital beds
by families, lovers and friends
and by the State releasing its paupers
for a life after death with purpose

with death they serve
a higher cause
knowledge and medicine?

no, above all to serve
the museum itself

the purpose of any collection
is in the collecting itself
the locked door completes
any collection

> RULE 4-8-4 section 2.1:
> DO NOT PUT A NAME TO A FACE
> DIRECT ALL SUCH IMAGININGS TO
> Level 7.

(x)

(On leaving the museum)

WARNING!

equipment in this building is
the property of the University
any person found removing any item
or found in possession of any item
who has not been duly authorised in
writing to remove such an item
may be prosecuted

container no's
68-139-361
429 and 532

ARE NO LONGER
ON DISPLAY

(rumour has it that they
were removed from display
as they closely resembled
the body parts of past
actual living people
for instance students began to note
similarities between no. 361
'the dissection of the left palm'
and the waving hand
of a dead prime minister once viewed
in a Cinetone newsreel)

this resulted in the following

WARNING! WARNING!

any person found in the possession
of knowledge of any item which
is not included in the catalogue shall be
deemed to be in possession of
unauthorised knowledge and shall
report to Level 7
where they will

be required to present themselves before
the Board of Directors
of the School of Medicine
and submit themselves for
further examination

A MEETING WITH
THE TOE-CUTTER

Waiting for My Father

Feeling the heavy air
of closing time
we wait for the silence
of the jukebox

his gold tooth shines
as he rock 'n' rolls
another woman across
the scuffs and scratches
of a dance

floral she spins all beauty
flashes of colour
end on end
beehive to high-heel
into his beer

taps shut down
he takes her hips
and winks his children home
with a fistful of coins and
fish and chips for six

Exhibition Hotel

I was sometimes afraid
of selling in the pubs
the saloon bar men
so much like my father

they pushed
and poured
their lager breath
all over you

women there were different
scented with heat
all bare skin
and bright floral dresses
soft rouged cheeks
and fat red lips

these women would force
a sixpence deeply
into my pants pocket
kiss my lips wet
and not concern themselves
with the newspaper

Michael

It is difficult to bring you back
here before me
so to conjure you
I return to the battered case
secreted beneath a bed

I touch you lightly
by sliding my hand
across the cool silk
of a yellow rocker shirt
I see your face baby smiling
innocent into the camera's eye
shooting you
and taking the bread board
in my hands
(sent home from Pentridge)
I finger deep scars

and sometimes I walk
along that laneway
behind the Rainbow Hotel
I look down for you
and listen for a whistle
of a bullet split
the night air

Ladies' Lounge

Straddled across laminex chairs
dragged from kitchens
into warm streets, these women
would drink shandies and smoke cork-
tips while the *Hit Parade* drifted

from the verandah
we'd rest along the bluestone gutter
listening to our mothers
singing Cilla Black
they would do nails
brush hair, touch each other
in light of the afternoon sun

A Meeting with the Toe-cutter

He tracks his man
from back lane to mattress
the prey wrestling
his troubles

the toe-cutter ropes and gags
proceeds with efficiency
working his way through skin
sinew and bone

he extracts a truth (of sorts)
and scrubs palms clean
the warming stain
of confessional blood

payday is a corner
nursing a glass
carefully eyeing a cigarette smoke
dance solo in an ashtray

a ready hand rests
in a jacket pocket
as a sharpened eye turns
to the opening

ACKNOWLEDGEMENTS

I would like to thank Kent MacCarter for supporting the bits and pieces of my poetic life with this publication of Broken Teeth. Although I once gave him a leg-up in his negotiation of a university system's bureaucratic maze, I did not expect a favour in return. But, as the saying goes, 'what goes around, comes around'.

'A Meeting with the Toe-cutter' appeared in *Antithesis*, vol. 15, 2005. 'The Anatomy Contraption' (ten poems on the science of anatomy) appeared in *Performing Hybridity*, edited by May Joseph and Jennifer Natalya Fink, New York University Performing Arts Department and University of Minnesota Press, 1999. 'Chroming' appeared in *Agenda*, vol. 41, 2005. 'Footnote to a History War' (archive box no. 2.)', appeared in *Meanjin*, no. 4, 2004. 'Mahzar' appeared in *Arena Magazine*, December–January, 2003-04. 'Ladies' Lounge' appeared in *The Road South*, Bengal Creations and Five Island Press, India, 2007. 'Michael' appeared in *The Literary Half-Yearly*, volume XXXVII, number 2, July 1996, edited by HH Anniah Gowda, The Institute of Commonwealth and American Studies and English Language, Mysore-12, India. 'Razor Wire Nation' appeared in *Overland*, March, 2003. 'Traces' appeared in Antithesis, vol. 12, 2002. 'Waiting for my Father' appeared in *Antithesis*, vol. 7, 1995.

Tony Birch writes poetry, short fiction, novels and essays. He is currently the inaugural Dr. Bruce MacGuinness Research Fellow at Victoria University.